Oklahoma
The Sooner State

Miriam Coleman

PowerKiDS
press.

New York

Published in 2011 by The Rosen Publishing Group, Inc.
29 East 21st Street, New York, NY 10010

First Edition

Editor: Joanne Randolph
Book Design: Greg Tucker
Layout Design: Kate Laczynski
Photo Researcher: Jessica Gerweck

Photo Credits: Cover © www.istockphoto.com/Amelia Painter; p. 5 J. Pat Carter/Getty Images; p. 7 © North Wind Picture Archives; p. 7 (inset) Transcendental Graphics/Getty Images; p. 9 © SuperStock; p. 11 © www.istockphoto.com/Michael Reeves; pp. 13, 22 (flower) Shutterstock.com; p. 15 Lester Lefkowitz/Getty Images; p. 17 Jeremy Woodhouse/Getty Images; p. 19 Sindre Ellingsen/Getty Images; p. 22 (tree) © www.istockphoto.com/Jay Lazarin; p. 22 (animal) © www.istockphoto.com/Sascha Burkard; p. 22 (bird) Jeremy Woodhouse/Getty Images; p. 22 (Woody Guthrie) Michael Ochs Archives/Getty Images; p. 22 (Ralph Ellison) Ben Martin/Time & Life Images/Getty Images; p. 22 (Carrie Underwood) Steve Granitz/WireImage/Getty Images.

Library of Congress Cataloging-in-Publication Data

Coleman, Miriam.
  Oklahoma : the Sooner State / by Miriam Coleman. — 1st ed.
     p. cm. — (Our amazing states)
  Includes index.
  ISBN 978-1-4488-0657-7 (library binding) — ISBN 978-1-4488-0746-8 (pbk.) —
ISBN 978-1-4488-0747-5 (6-pack)
  1. Oklahoma—Juvenile literature. I. Title.
  F694.3.C65 2011
  976.6—dc22

                                    2009052014

Manufactured in the United States of America

CPSIA Compliance Information: Batch #WS10PK: For Further Information contact Rosen Publishing, New York, New York at 1-800-237-9932

Contents

Racing into the Sooner State

On the day that Oklahoma was opened for settlement, **pioneers** lined up by the thousands to move onto the **fertile** land. When the shot was fired to **signal** that settlement could begin, people raced in to claim the best land. Oklahoma is known as the Sooner State because some settlers slipped in to claim a spot "sooner" than the land was officially opened. Today farms and oil and natural gas wells can be seen across the state.

Shaped like a pan, Oklahoma sits right near the middle of the United States. The name Oklahoma comes from two Choctaw Indian words meaning "red people." Oklahoma is home to the largest Native American population in the United States.

Here a man wears Native American clothing during a festival in Oklahoma. More than 25 Native American languages are spoken in Oklahoma.

From Indian Territory to Statehood

Long before Oklahoma joined the United States, the land was home to the Arapaho, Caddo, Cheyenne, Comanche, Kiowa, Osage, Pawnee, and Wichita Indians. Between 1830 and 1842, the United States forced other Native American tribes from the Southeast, including the Choctaws, Seminoles, and Cherokees, to move to Oklahoma. This forced journey is known as the Trail of Tears because so many people died on the trip.

The Indians were promised that they would own all the land in Oklahoma. The U.S. government later bought much of the land from the Indians. In 1889, Oklahoma was opened for white settlement. Oklahoma became the forty-sixth state in 1907.

Settlers rush into Oklahoma territory in 1889. *Inset*: This map of Indian Territory dates from 1890. It shows where different Native American groups had settled.

Cherokee Heritage Center

Before Oklahoma became a state, each Native American nation had its own independent government. Tahlequah, Oklahoma, was the capital of the Cherokee Nation. If you visit Tahlequah today, you can still find the red brick Cherokee National Capitol Building, the Cherokee Supreme Court Building, and the Cherokee National Prison. Many signs in the town are printed in the Cherokee language.

The nearby Cherokee **Heritage** Center can teach you even more about the tribe. Model villages show what Cherokee life was like at different times in history. You can learn about Cherokee crafts and see furniture and animals that were carried to Oklahoma on the Trail of Tears.

This medicine man does his work at the Tsa-La-Gi Ancient Village, at the Cherokee Heritage Center. People can see what Cherokee life was like during the 1600s there.

9

From the Mountains to the Prairies

Oklahoma has many different kinds of land. On the eastern side of the state, the Ozark **Plateau**, the **Prairie** Plains, and the Ouachita Mountains form the border between Oklahoma, Arkansas, and Missouri. Oklahoma also has the Arbuckle and Wichita mountains and the Gypsum Hills. Black Mesa, at 4,973 feet (1,516 km), is the state's highest point. It rises from the tall, grassy High Plains in northwest Oklahoma. Much of Oklahoma's land is made up of the Red Bed Plains.

Oklahoma has rivers, too. The Red River winds along the bottom of the state, and the Arkansas River flows through the northeast. The **climate** in Oklahoma is mostly warm and dry, but the state is sometimes hit by storms and even **tornadoes**.

This is a view from Mount Scott. You can see the flat prairies that go on for miles from there. Mount Scott is part of the Wichita Mountains.

Where the Buffalo Roam

Because Oklahoma has so many different kinds of land, it grows many kinds of plants. Lots of different animals live there, too. Trees such as ashes, hickories, elms, walnuts, sweet gums, and pines grow in Oklahoma's forests. Deer, mink, and foxes make their homes among these trees.

On the prairies, you can find grasses, such as bluestem, Indian grass, and buffalo grass. Coyotes, prairie dogs, and armadillos make their homes there.

Oklahoma's state animal is the American bison. Thousands of these huge animals once **grazed** on the Great Plains. People hunted the bison so much they almost disappeared. Oklahoma has now brought the animal back to places like the Tallgrass Prairie Preserve, though.

American bison are the largest land animals in North America. They can be up to 6 feet (2 m) tall at the shoulder and can weigh up to 2,000 pounds (907 kg)!

Ranches and Oil Wells of Oklahoma

Oil and natural gas are big business in Oklahoma. They can be found in nearly every county in the state. You can see oil and gas wells pumping all over Oklahoma's landscape.

Farming is also important. In fact, three-quarters of Oklahoma's land is used for farms. Oklahoma is one of the top states in the country for growing wheat and rye. Oklahoma farmers also grow lots of peanuts, corn, pecans, and peaches. Oklahoma's biggest farm **product** is beef. Oklahoma is famous for the white-faced cattle that graze on its ranches.

Aviation, which has to do with planes and flying, and biotechnology are other important businesses in Oklahoma. Biotechnology is a field that combines biology, food science, medicine, and farming.

This oil derrick stands over an oil well in an Oklahoma field. An oil derrick is used to drill down to the oil, but it is not used to pump the oil out of the ground.

A Look at Oklahoma City

Oklahoma's capital is Oklahoma City. It is the biggest city in Oklahoma and one of the biggest cities by land area in the United States. Oklahoma City lies along the North Canadian River, in the middle of Oklahoma. The land where Oklahoma City is now was opened for settlement on April 22, 1889. In the morning of that day, it was empty prairie. By the evening, there were 10,000 people living there! Oklahoma City became the state capital in 1910.

One of the largest oil fields in the country lies beneath Oklahoma City's soil. There is even an oil well on the statehouse lawn. Oklahoma City has a lot to see and do. You can even take a water taxi through its Bricktown neighborhood.

Oklahoma City has a lot to offer people who live there, such as museums, theaters, a zoo, and more. Many businesses have headquarters in the city as well.

Remembering a Western Past

When Oklahoma was still Indian Territory, cowboys would drive great herds of cattle across the land from Texas up to the railroads in Kansas. Cowboys became an important part of the **culture** in Oklahoma. Their skills at roping cattle are still celebrated at big events like the International Finals Rodeo, in Oklahoma City.

You can learn more about cowboys and Oklahoma pioneers at the National Cowboy and Western Heritage Museum, in Oklahoma City. You can look at paintings of the old West or learn about the history of cowboys, **saddles**, and **spurs**. You can even visit a model of a cattle town from the early 1900s!

The National Cowboy and Western Heritage Museum opened its doors in 1955. It is a great place to learn about the history of the American West.

Visiting the Sooner State

Oklahoma is a land of cowboys and Indians and of big cities and open ranges. You can learn all about pioneer and Native American history there. You can also enjoy the beauty of the natural landscape. Oklahoma has seven different mountain ranges as well as wonderful state parks, such as Beaver's Bend and Lake Wister. The city of Guthrie has 160 historic buildings. The Oklahoma National Stockyards, in Oklahoma City, is one of the world's biggest cattle markets!

With all Oklahoma has to offer, you can see why some settlers wanted to get there sooner than the others. Now, you can take your time and get to know Oklahoma at your own pace.

Glossary

climate (KLY-mit) The kind of weather a certain area has.

culture (KUL-chur) The beliefs, practices, and arts of a group of people.

fertile (FER-tul) Good for making and growing things.

grazed (GRAYZD) Fed on grass.

heritage (HER-uh-tij) The stories and ways of doing things that are handed down from parent to child.

pioneers (py-uh-NEERZ) Some of the first people to settle in a new area.

plateau (pla-TOH) A broad, flat, high piece of land.

prairie (PRER-ee) A large area of flat land with grass but few or no trees.

product (PRAH-dukt) Something that is made.

saddles (SA-dulz) Leather seats that are used on the backs of horses to carry riders.

signal (SIG-nul) To make a movement or sound that gives a message.

spurs (SPURZ) Spikes worn on a rider's heel to make a horse go faster.

tornadoes (tor-NAY-dohz) Funnel-shaped clouds of wind in which strong, fast winds spin around a center.

Oklahoma State Symbols

State Tree
Redbud

State Animal
American Bison

OKLAHOMA

State Flag

State Bird
Scissor-Tailed
Flycatcher

State Wildflower
Indian Blanket

State Seal

Famous People from Oklahoma

Woody Guthrie
(1912–1967)
Born in Okemah, OK
Folksinger

Ralph Ellison
(1914–1994)
Born in Oklahoma
City, OK
Author

Carrie Underwood
(1983–)
Born in Checotah, OK
Country Singer/
Songwriter

Oklahoma State Map

Legend
○ Major City

⭐ Capital

〰 River

Ozark Plateau

Tulsa

Broken Arrow

Edmond

Muskogee

Canadian River

Elk City

Oklahoma City

Norman

Arkansas River

Wichita Mountains

Eufaula Lake

Lawton

Arbuckle Mountains

Ouachita Mountains

Red River

Lake Texoma

Oklahoma State Facts

Population: About 3,547,884

Area: 68,667 square miles (177,847 sq km)

Motto: "Labor Omnia Vincit" (Labor Conquers All Things)

Song: "Oklahoma!," from the Rodgers and Hammerstein musical of the same name

Index

Web Sites

Due to the changing nature of Internet links, PowerKids Press has developed an online list of Web sites related to the subject of this book. This site is updated regularly. Please use this link to access the list:

www.powerkidslinks.com/amst/ok/